OUR CHICAGO
faces and voices of the city

Richard Younker

CHICAGO REVIEW PRESS

Library of Congress Cataloging-in-Publication Data

Younker, Richard.
   Our Chicago.

   1. Chicago (Ill.)—Description—1981-   —Views.
2. Chicago (Ill.)—Biography—Portraits.   I. Title.
F548.37.Y68   1987   977.3'1104'0922 [B]   87-29906
ISBN 1-55652-022-0 (pbk.)

Printed in the United States of America

First edition

Published by Chicago Review Press, Incorporated,
   814 N. Franklin, Chicago, IL 60610

To my father

Acknowledgments

Much gratitude to Barbara Smetzer for her long-time interest in the project and for her insightful advice concerning both the photos and the text (often interrupting her own work to give same). Her encouragement and attention helped me more than she realizes.

Thanks to Janet Davis for a sympathetic ear and discerning assistance with the text.

Many thanks to the people in this book who allowed me to photograph them and who shared their words and their lives with me.

Thanks to Sylvester Finley, who, my first day working at the post office, on hearing I was a college grad said, "He's got a degree, now he's going to get an education."

Thanks to Jack Leblebijian, of Gamma Photo Labs of Chicago, who was sensitive to my preferences in printing.

And special thanks to Mrs. Lindy Bergman and Mrs. Beatrice Younker.

Thanks to Curt Matthews, who has always believed in this book, and to Linda Matthews, whose recent editorial direction strengthened and pulled it together.

And many thanks to the staff at the now defunct *Midwest Magazine*, the *Chicago Sun-Times* Sunday magazine: Ed Spivey, who published my first photo essay, Tony Monahan, Tom Burnison, and Dick Takeuchi, who all encouraged me to follow my photographic instincts and provided a showplace for the results, and Bob Bradford, who gives me a hug and tells me how great I am at Tony's Christmas parties.

A Note From the Author

This book was fifteen years in the making. I took the photographs between 1972 and 1987 in the Chicago area, from Albany Park and Uptown on the north to the Calumet River and East Chicago on the south; from the Loop and lakefront west to Humboldt Park and Bensenville, with a little jaunt up northwest to Arlington Heights.

Virtually all the photographs represent hours I stole from my work as a commercial photojournalist, days when I left my apartment with two cameras slung around my neck, ready to roam and explore wherever I liked. On these occasions I feel like a discoverer of new lands, so fresh to me are the lives of those I am photographing.

The people whose portraits you see here were surprisingly open with me. Not only did they allow me to photograph them, but they often sat and shared their thoughts with me, or at least shouted them over their shoulders during the working day. Perhaps their openness was a consequence of my enthusiasm; perhaps the subjects were flattered by the attention of my camera, or maybe both or neither.

In any case, from my conversations with them came the monologues that accompany many of the photographs. I have taken the liberty of matching one person's words with another's portrait, as I photographed and listened to many different people at each location.

Thumbnail Sketch

I'll give you a thumbnail sketch of Artie.
Allright, he's a hustler, you know that.
And to make a roll he's got to ride
the circuit, so to speak. Play the strange towns,
the small towns; walk into rooms where there are guys
who'll break his fingers if they think he hustled them.
That takes a lot of guts. And Artie doesn't
have 'em. There's nothing wrong with that.
You don't and neither do I, I'm too old.
So how well can he do in the local pool room here?

Okay, now he's makin' a little book,
he's takin' some bets on the side.
Doin' pretty good too. But not too good. Oh, no.
Who do you think runs these off track joints?
Not independents like you or I, Dick. Of course.
First day these two big guys walk through the door:
"We wanna talk to the owner." Wham! Bam!
The BACK-of-the-hand, the SLAP-of-the-hand!
"And you better not open tomorrow neither."

So that's Artie Dabromowicz.
And did you know that he can't read or write?

Industrial truck cleaner

1400 N. Magnolia, July 1978

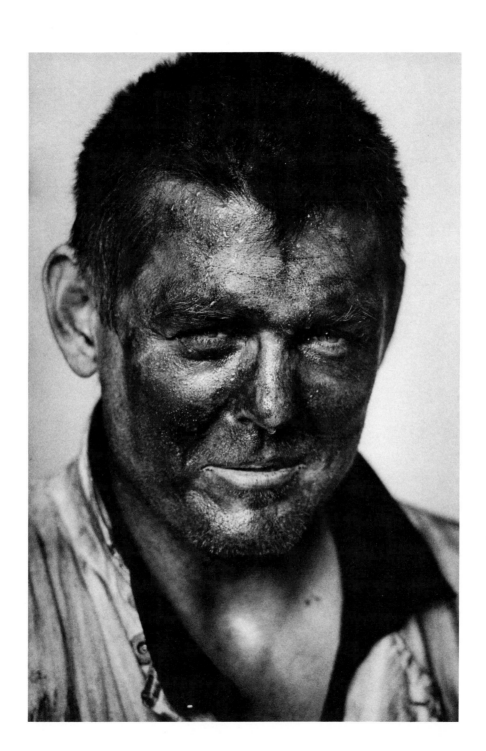

Dominoes

Humboldt Park, July 1976

Salvage

I can make forty a day. Even forty-five, fifty. Sometime only net eighteen. That's okay too. 'Cause there's money out there. Oh yeah. Someone pass by this and all he see's a vacant lot. House knocked down. Another person, someone used to salvage, he see a gold mine.

Some of these young fellas haul off a hundred, hundred fifty a day. A day! But next time you see 'em, they broke. Stop you on the street, "Hey, Jimmy, you got a quarter?" I mean I'm fifty-eight years old; I go out and work six days a week.

But if you can't find a job, you got to scuffle. What I call myself doin' out here. An' I do allright. I do ALLright. Aluminum is fifty cent a pound, brass'll get you twenty-seven, copper's about fifteen; cast iron don't bring but two and a half. But it's good. When you ain't got nothin', it's all good.

Miss Oh-So-Tired

We'd work from can see to can't.
Go out when it was just light enough to see shapes
and then keep on 'til way pas' dinner. It be
so dark they had to weigh the bales by candlelight.

All day long in that field. All DAY long! So hot
you could see monkeys jumpin'. And then the hay
catch fire. No, I ain't jokin'. Down South
they used to grow this wheat straw. Set it out in piles
to dry, but after 'while the sun get so strong
on it, it just whoosh up in flames. Start
burnin' and wouldn't be a match for miles around.
Then everything go up. Acres and acres!

When I was fo'teen I told my momma,
I said, "Momma, one day I'm gonna leave Mississippi."
She say, "Oh, girl, you get used to it."
I said, "No, momma! I don't care if I have
to ride the back of a mule or if I have
to go walkin', but I'm gonna LEAVE Mississippi:"

But honestly, I don't think young people today
knows what hard work is. I'm tellin' you! It's like
my daughter. Sometime I jus' don't understand her, Richard!
I mean she graduate high school and she have
a good job, It's nothin' hard; she just sit
up in a office six or seven hours.
But on Sunday when I ax her do she want
to go to church, she say, "Oh, momma, I'm
so tired." I say, "Okay, Miss Oh-So-Tired!"

Stockton Drive and Fullerton Street, October 1973

Be Proud

At work the prejudice is very bad.
The whites don't recognize the Mexicans,
they won't say nothin' to 'em at all.
I'm the only Mexican with skills,
but I'm polite, I say good morning to
the foreman, everybody there, but all
of them just turn their heads.

And this American, I think he come from
some European country, he showed me how
repairs supposed to go. But if
the sequence went from A to B to C
he did it just the other way around.
I knew what he was doin', but we have
machines I'd never seen in school;
although I could have done all right if I
just do the opposite of what he tells me.
But then I said to him, "John, if Gerhardt
(our boss) asks me to do repairs and it
don't work out right, I'm gonna tell him that
I couldn't learn because you showed me wrong,
you tried to foul me up on purpose." After
that everything's okay. He respected me.
Next day big smile, "Good morning, Hector." Yeah,
"Good morning, John."

But that's the way it is
with these people. You gotta be tough with them.
I'm not a fist fighter or nothin' like that,
but I stand up to people. You have to. Of course.
I never tell my kids about too much of this stuff.
What for? Oh I might say a little. But mostly
I tell them to be proud. Be proud of what you are.

Southern Ways

I don't know what it is, the city'll turn a man against his brother. Back South it's so relaxed. We never locked our door or took our keys out of the ignition. Never thought about it. But in this here Uptown, boy, it's something else.

Might have some fella over to the house, a guy you thought was your friend. After a while you excuse yourself, you know, and by the time you pulled your zipper up, he done cleaned out your apartment. So help me. Probably happened to everyone of us standing here. Maybe only once, but it did. I sure do miss them Southern ways.

"I was the man . . ."

That's what I boxed as, a lightweight, just like
Jesse here. And I fought the best, Rich.
I fought 'em all. Scrapped Johnny Bratton for
the title. Twice. Almost had him one time.
Do you know I was the first man to knock
Johnny Bratton down? That's right. Oh, he
just hated to fight me! Back then I was
a boxer, see, fight weekends, but I danced
some too. On Friday nights I put on exhibitions
in clubs. Do Charleston, a little soft-shoe,
tap dance. And Johnny Bratton couldn't hit me, see,

come out his corner throwing punches, see, just like
a windmill (oh, him and that Beau Jack
was murder if they ever catch you!) bull out,
but now I'd pick 'em off like this, whap-whap,
or do a little shuffle step and slip away
like this here, maybe sting him one.

He'd be so frustrated. And then one time,
his trainer told me this, he got
so mad the tears rolled down his cheeks.
They did. Mmhmm. Because of me. Yes sir,
I was the man that made Johnny Bratton cry.

Innocent

We joined the Gaylords about three years ago.
Before that, everybody was doing it,
I don't know why, we were in
the Royals. Before that we were innocent.

Initiation

. . . you can defend yourself, put up your hands
or move around, but it ain't gonna do
no good, 'cause they be comin' at you
with everything they got. They hit your face,
your chest, just about anyplace. But if you take it,
if you still standing after thirty seconds, you a
Disciple. That's how you join.

To get out? I don't even want to think about it.

"... he won't look me in the face."

Check out the Polack, the guy with the scarf around his head. That's where he took a bullet. I still don't know how he lived, man. I wonder who got him, don't you, Alvin? Heh, heh. See him stare down at the sidewalk! Yeah, he won't look me in the face. Punk.

Street Gang Leader

My name's Ray. They call me Mister Future, you
probably read about me in the papers. See,
I've stomped a lot of people, I've offed
a lot of people, and never gone to jail
or nothin'. But, now everyone around here says
it's gonna happen: someone's gonna do me in later on.
That's why they call me Mister Future . . . yeah.

"I thought these people were hicks . . ."

You know what? In the gangs you don't have any friends. It's everyone for himself. They shoot you in the back if you don't watch out. They take your girlfriend. Sure, guys in your own gang.

I used to be president of the Latin Disciples. And like my members, I thought these people were hicks, singing hallelujah, glory to God, and all that. But then one day I said, why not give them a try? Because I wasn't going anywhere.

Hey, who needs a forty-five to be macho? I'm much more a man for following the Lord.

Beloved Pan, and all ye other gods
that haunt this place,
give me beauty of the inward soul;
and may the outer and the inner man be at one.

—Socrates

Signals

It sure was a lot more interesting before
they put in their "communications."
We used to be able to say almost anything by gesture.
Take numbers: for one you just clap once, for two
it's twice, five was a fist, and if
you touched your belt, the elbows out, why that
was eight. Reclining, see? Locations too.
To send a hogger to the pocket, say,
first motion him away, then brush the side
of your pants. You touch your pocket. For
the ice house, get him goin' again, and blow into
your hands, like when it's cold outside. Oh yeah,
we had a lot of fun with all our signals!
Back then. But now you switch on
the radio, "One forty-seven, shove
'em in the clear!" A lot of static too.

Pile Driver

I started out as pile driver t'irdy years ago.
After t'ree months I get a bad headache. So
I go to see this doctor in Hahmund, Indiana
where I was working. He say, "What you do
for a living?" I say, "Operate a pile driver."
He say, "You know how to cure them headaches? Find
another job." So I get on as carpenter about six months.
But dot give out so I go back to da pile driver.
And dot's da way it's been. A little bit o' carpenter,
a little bit o' pile driving; back and forth, back and forth.

I worked on dot filtration plant out at Navy Pier.
You know how many piles they got to drive out there?
A hundred fifty t'ousand! What a racket dey make, you don't
believe it! Now my right ear's dead, don't hear nothin',
and in da left is just a little when I turn up machine.
Today dey got dese plugs, but I never did like 'em.

Ironworker

Me n' Joe work in rain, snow, everything.
On days so cold you won't see no one
walkin' outdoors, not even between
buildings, we're out here fourteen, sixteen hours.
All the other tradesmen go home. We stay.

Truck Driver

Three words I used to hate the most
were, go to work. "I've got to go to work.
It's eleven o'clock I've got to get some sleep
so I can get up and go to work." Huh-uh.
See, I'll be at work. I'd live the job for two,
three weeks at a stretch. Like shoot to Baton Rouge,
take on a load and come straight back to Memphis. Knowin'
I couldn't sleep for fifty hours never bothered me.
Just don't make me run by someone else's schedule.

Waitin' for loads down South I'd miss a day
and fish. You got a frying pan and then
I'd keep a long stick of butter in
the cooler with my emergency rations.
Drive down a side road and maybe catch dinner.
Live off the land. It's like my mother said,
"Truck driver's nothing but a hobo who's got a job."

Kaaah-chug

If you wanted to see something special,
it had to be an engineer on one
of the old steam engines. They had romance
on the railroad back then. When I come on in '48
I fired for this great, big Italian fellow
with one of them handlebar mustaches.
Oh, he run a tight ship, no questions asked.
I'd report half hour early on his crew.
Sweep the floor, every cinder, ash and bit
of dust, polish the windows, and rub
them grab rails 'til they shone.

Back then you dressed
like railroaders, too. It was a uniform.
Everybody wore the coveralls,
and you remember them red bandannas?
They kept the cinders from falling down our shirts.
You could get a nasty burn from one of them.
Scorch you! So before getting on the train,
we'd take the kerchief, tie it real tight
around our necks and fasten it with a safety pin.
That was the dress code. Now this here I got on
is casual, I'd wear it to the bowling alley.
See, you don't even get dirty on the job anymore!

And the diesel that we got today
is much smoother: everything in one long,
even, level draw. Like drivin' a car
with automatic trans. Nothin' to it.
But not the steamers. No sir! Like takin' that seven
mile stretch of hill goin' into Milwaukee. You couldn't
just glide up it. Had to take it real easy:
kaaah-chug, kaaah-chug, kaaaaah-chug.
Although on level ground
there was nothing stronger. Why, if you tied the Rocky Mountains
onto an old S-2, say, it'd haul 'em right into
the Rio Grande. Huh. Like a draft horse pullin' a kiddy wagon.

But uphill that was the best them pistons could do.
Kaaah-chug, kaaah-chug, we'd throttle down—whoosh!—just
over the line, kaaaaaaah-chug, through all seven miles of grade.
Ohhh, it was a thing of real beauty!

Ship's Cook

I've piloted boats so slow they couldn't get
out of their own way. But this one's a honey.
Twenty-one hundred horse on her. Engine alone
cost a quarter of a million dollars. On a quiet day
we'll tie on fourteen barges and take 'em over to Beth'.

But I'll tell you one thing: if you get a good cook,
you better pamper the piss out of him. 'Cause
he's worth his weight in gold, you better believe it!
You know the politician, Bill O'Connor? His brother,
Jack, used to be our cook. Goddamn good one too!
I mean he kept his galley clean. I
wouldn't be afraid to have my men chow off a'
the floor, that's how clean he kept it.
But that guy could cook and I mean everything.

But there was one thing Jack liked
more than anything else in the world. Casino.
With the two of spades and the ten of diamonds. If you
played casino with Jack, you'd eat good, man, I swear it.

You know that landfill at Northwestern
University, with the park and the
observatory? We brought all that sand up there.
Worked 'round the clock: fourteen days on, seven
days off. Played a lotta casino on those hauls.
And had steak every night. You better believe it!

Heights

Bein' up here has no effect on me at all.
What makes it easy is if you work your way up.
On the first floor you look over the side,
and that's nothin'. Second floor's the same.
And so forth. We put up a building on North Lake
Shore Drive and when we got to the fortieth floor
I looked down to the ground one day and shouted, "Hey!
we need some iron," or I don't know, maybe
it was, "Stacks up here!" Of course there was no way
they could hear me, even through a bullhorn, with
the wind blowin' and everything. But you get
so used to it, the goin' up floor by floor, that when
you reach the top, it's like stoppin' at the edge of the curb.
As if you're shakin' hands with the earth almost.

Brickchip

This just a little piece a job I got. Hard?
You bet it's hard work! First you gotta find
the bricks, then you gotta clean 'em,
and lastly stack 'em up.

'N these bricks here is bad. Almost all
of 'em you gotta knock something off.
'N that hurt your hand. It hurt
your wrist, it hurt your arms, it even go
down into your legs. 'N what with
the rain we had, it makes 'em heavy as
they are again. Yeah. Again and again!

Montrose and Broadway, July 1978

Dewey: You need a drink, Bob?
Bob: No I don't . . . but I will.

Garbage Picker

I know what's going on with these rich people, man.
Go to Treasure Island, buy 'em ninety dollars worth
of groceries. Get home, look inside
the bag an' if they don't like the wrapper
or somethin' . . . out she goes. Oh yeah, you'd be
surprised at what they throw away! Meat. Vegetables.
Whole loaves of bread. Not stale.
Braaand new. But, hey, it's rough out here.
These people may not know it, man, hard times
is just around the corner.

Unopened. Loaves and loaves.
And then one day they gonna wish they had a slice.

Jug and a Pack of Smokes

Been sittin' on this bench since nine o'clock.
This wine ain't got no kick to it. Just makes
you feel real dizzy. I only had a dollar
eighty-five this morning, couldn't afford no whiskey.

We used to sneak across to Mexico. Juarez.
Shack up, you know. You ever been to Mexico?
Better not go alone or if you do,
you better get yourself together. They'll throw
you in the jug first thing. And then the judge
'll go evaluate your car. And that's a known fact.

I got a dollar forty-one now with
the quarter that you give me. I think I'll go get
a jug and a pack of smokes, although
this port won't pick you up none, know what I mean?

I 'as sleepin' in a hallway just yesterday,
couple police came in and say, "Get out
of here, you Irish prick!" Now what they want
a call me that for? I ain't done nothin'.

Street Talk

You may not know this, see, but a alcoholic
never hurt nobody. Harmless. We're mellow people, man.
But a dope fiend is something else. Look out!

But we all friends out here. I got a white
friend. I call him honky-donkey, he calls
me nigger. 'Cause we friends. Don't nobody care
about color. Only color we think
about's the color of the wine. Ain't that right,
brother? This' John, th' only white alcoholic on
the street. Gimme a cigarette there, John.

Ain't that right what I been tellin' him, John?
Alcoholic never hurt a flea.
No, no, okay, a blackout then he ain't himself.
Like me or John get sick, instead of goin' to
a hospital or have a wife who tend to us
at home, we might lay down in the middle of
the street here. Allright . . . and that's a death bed.

Randolph Street Market Boss

It's all very friendly, like a community. Weekends we have all the beautiful shoppers, the housewives. One Saturday a truck driver came in from California and starts talkin' to one of our lady customers. Next thing you know they go to City Hall. Get married. After they know each other one hour! Then they come back and we throw a party for them right here in this building.

Boatyard laborer

Chicago River at Belmont, October 1973

Local 1

    We're in Local 1, structural ironworkers. Weld and burn.
Mostly supports and railing on railroad bridges. Maybe a wreck
damaged 'em or they just rusted out with age. Like this one that
run over the Mississippi at Hannibal, Missouri. Stayed on that job
seven months. S'real pretty down there. Reminded me of my
hometown, Rosiclare, in southern Illinois. You never heard of it?
Oh, it's a big one. All of about fifteen hundred people.

Fulton Street Market

I can't describe the action here. You have to live it really. Trucks unloading, trucks waiting to get at the docks, customers in a hurry for their orders . . .

Street Pavers

Don't stand between the machine and the truck!
They had a guy on last year got hit by the pan
and fell underneath the roller. When
Don pulled away he was lying there.
It crushed his chest. Just moved his lips
a little bit, asked for a drink of water, and died.

But I'm like this, see, watching. I'm watching,
I'm watching, I'm watching . . . we watch for each other.

Lakewood Sluggers

Near Lakewood and Wellington, August 1975

Railbird

The first thing I look for in a horse
is balance. Like that one over there. He's got
a nice, full, rounded ass, but his back slopes up.
His head's held high. That's a very nice horse.

And I want a high flesh. His coat should be smooth
and full. Then I know the grooms are taking care
of him. He isn't backing off his feed. I don't
want moisture on his legs. Very bad.
They got him standing up to here in ice water.
That means arthritis or maybe even foundering.

Next I want him big. Even a little fat
won't bother me. Because these horses
not only run a distance, they carry weight
across it. They're not race horses. Work
animals. Oxen. When I hear a trainer say his horse
is putting on pounds during the campaign . . .
Okay, they're starting . . . look in front . . . you see
my pony's forelegs hit the ground together . . . that's
an athlete . . . money in the bank if he
holds stride . . . let me touch you for luck, babe.

Tommy's

A tradesman get laid off, 'bout all he had to do
was go to Tommy's Bar and find an empty stool.
Be sociable. "Say, what's your trade?" they'd ask him.
And, "Wasn't you on the Hancock Building? Come
on over and meet the foreman!"
Of course it didn't hurt to have a name
like Petersen or Jensen. Or O'Brien.

Fact I'd say more buildings went up in Tommy's than all
the drafting boards and executive offices combined.

Taxi

Me n' my old lady been together
twenty-two years. Now she's not beautiful.
Won't turn no heads when she walk down the street.
But she does have a nice body. A big body. I like
a woman with a big body. I'm a big man
and she's a big woman. We go well together.
She's nice too, has a pleasant personality,
and that's the most important thing. She's fun
to be around. We enjoy each other.
See, we lovers AND we friends.

Now this buddy of mine, I've known him
since high school, he likes the young women.
He been runnin' around with this gal,
she's twenty-nine years old. He's sixty.
He gotta take her to the nightclub
two, three times a week, buy her all kind
expensive clothes, and then they went out to
the showroom Christmas Eve to pick her out a brand new ride.

I see him with his lady now. And she is
attractive. She has a gorgeous face. But I ask myself,
just who's he tryin' to impress? And does
he really like her? More to the point, does she really
like him? Or how long will she stay home
and watch TV the nights he's too beat to go
out cabareting? It ain't none of my business, see, I just
say at my age I don't need the aggravation.

My wife's the only thing that keep me out
on these streets. Weren't for her I would have shut off
this meter a long time ago. But at fifty-six
what else m' I gonna do? I'm stuck. Everyday
twelve hours of fightin' traffic, duckin' the POlice.
Ain't nothin' I can't handle, but quittin' time
you walk in the house, fall back on the sofa, put up
your feet, look down and find you got a drink in both hands.

Yardmaster

You know I just can't understand people that don't like
their work. How can someone get out of bed every morning
and go to something that they hate? Because
I get a bang out of this job. Mmhmm.
Yeah, me and the railroad get along real well.
I do the work and they pay me. Plus I get good benefits.

But it'd be hard explaining this to an outsider.
Well, take my next door neighbor. He's got a
big model train setup in his basement, probably
ten thousand dollars worth of equipment. It takes
up the whole area. Now he'll go down there and spend
a weekend, hardly see his wife and children
for forty-eight hours straight. Just like an overgrown kid.

Oh, he's got everything: switch engines, sidings,
waycars, covered hoppers, the works. And that's fine.
For him. But I don't need it. Uh-uh. You know why?
Because I've got the real thing, right out here in the yard.

Politicoes

Don't think Chicago has a lock on colorful politicoes. No sir. Because the Talmadges of Georgia, my home state, give ground to none in that department. Take Eugene: Harvard Law Degree, brilliant, and a voice like William Jennings Bryan, but when he spoke to his constituents it was all backwoods and homespun. Proud papa'd introduce junior, say, "This my son, Hummin Tummidge." Hummin Tummidge, just like he'd been drinkin corn liquor with the boys behind the grocery.

And he used to end every speech the same. It was almost like a trademark with him. He'd say, "The poah mayun in Jawjuh has three friends in this world: Jesus Christ, Sears Roebuck and Eugene Talmadge!"

420 to 8 Man

You hear what the committeeman called me last night? Said I'm an "old 420 to 8 man." That's right, if the opposition gets fifteen votes in my precinct it's an upset. In '58 we carried four oh nine to two. I just lose the Republican judges and even they apologize for goin' against me. "What the hell!" I told 'em, "we don't want no investigation out here. Vote your conscience."

Of course how would they know I could change their ballots on the way to headquarters. Oh, Jesus! you know we'd take the box home sometimes and mark 'em up. But you had to be real careful with them erasures. That's why it took all night. And then next morning throw down a cup of hot coffee and drive the tallies over to Clark Street. All for the party of justice and mercy.

I mean there I am in '33, dead broke, holes in my shoes, no food in the cupboard and they took me aboard. Been on the payroll forty-two years. And that's no one-night stand now, Joe, is it?

John Henry Davis, Street Musician

Now all my people musicians. My daddy was
a awgan player, my mamma was a shake dancer in
a church. Lightnin' Hopkin' Davis, he
my uncle. Sammy Davis Jr., he born
'back of a show wagon, Loozeyanna. Sho' wa'. He kin too.

Now I don't got no education. Can't read
no music. What fah? What I gotta read it fah?
I hear somethin', I play it. Somebody burn
that book a' music, then what you gonna do?
'Thout all them notes you lost, ain't you? But I
was raised in music; it somethin' have
to be inside you, somethin' y'ave to feel,
to feel the beat. All th'education in
the world can't help you with that. Ain't that right?

My own boss. Don't have to stick my nose up
nobody' beehind. Do I? I tell the band
what time to start and when I tell 'em to quit,
they quits. Anybody else tell 'em what time? Tell
'em what to play too. Didn't go past the fou'th grade
and my own boss. Contractor too. Do paintin',
decoratin', and construction. Thirty-nine
years old and never worked for nobody else a day in my life!

That way I be raised. My mother told me, say,
"John Henry, ain't nobody gonna gi'
you nothin' in this world; just one person you
can 'pend on and that you'self." And I
work seven days a week. Get up six o'clock in
the mornin', every mornin'; ever'body else
be 'sleep, the kids, the wife . . . I step over 'em, make
my own breakfast and go on out the house.

Watch Repairman

I grew up on the North Side. My parents were both from the old country, and even though I was born in Chicago I only spoke German until the age of five. Funny thing, you could walk through entire neighborhoods, certainly ours, and never hear a word of English.

Flower vendor

Corner of Fullerton and Racine, October 1978

Cubans making cigars in their kitchen

2900 W. George, October 1973

Pumpkin Salesmen

But, oh, the people, God love 'em. They see us in
our coveralls and right away
you know what comes into their minds: farmer . . . dumb.
Hell! we're part of the display. Two Santa Clauses.
And then we got our cornstalks stacked up nice,
the bushel baskets filled with fruit
and taffy apples for the little ones.
So if the public wants to think we're country,
let 'em. Don't hurt nothin'. Come one,
come all. Welcome. Everybody welcome!

Reminiscences

I knew Billy Sunday. You know he used to be
a ballplayer. Played for the Cubs only they called
'em something else back then. And for
a while there he was a down and outer. That's right,
we had a tailor shop and run a little second
hand store on Harrison. He'd come in and pawn
his clothes, even his shoes sometime, to buy
a pint of whiskey. Sure, sure. Hung around
so much one time my father called me over,
said, "Abe, here's a dollar, take this fellow to
the mission, and see he gets a place to stay.
'Cause he's driving me crazy!"

You know I grew up next door to Hinky Dink?
The alderman. Him and the other fellow, now what's
his name . . . Bathhouse John. They traded off
every two years in the city council.
You hear of his Workingman's Bar? Why, he
had the riff-raff from all over the city sleeping in
that place, every kind of tramp imaginable.
Fed 'em real good, see. Then six
o'clock election day, they'd throw a string
of firecrackers in the basement there.

Now I remember they had them great, big schooners with
the thick bottoms, real heavy. And Jesus! you had
to watch out in there! Sure! Why, anytime
you turned your head another bum'd grab your glass!

You ever hear of the Yellow Kid? The celebrated
Yellow Kid Weil. Did I know him! We were like this!

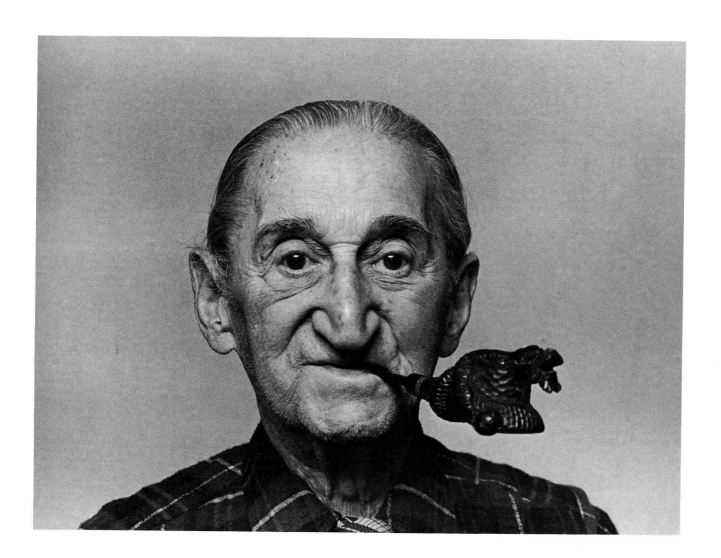

A Gentleman's Game

You see, billiards is a gentleman's game:
"How do you do, sir?" Sir! In pool
it's, "Ah, you son of a bitch!"
Proprietor says, "Sudakis, you think
you could watch the language, uh, there's
a lady present?" "Aw, go fuck yourself!"
Now how can you take your wife to a place like that!

List of Photographs

Title and Date   Page

1400 N. Magnolia July 1978 11
Humboldt Park June 1976 13
Buena and Sheridan July 1978 15
Jamaica January 1973 17
Stockton Drive and Fullerton Street October 1973 19
Lincoln Park Zoo October 1973 21
Magnolia and Wilson August 1978 23
1700 W. Addison February 1975 25
Kedzie and North Avenue March 1975 27
1700 W. Addison February 1975 29
4600 N. Magnolia July 1978 31
1500 N. Damen September 1985 33
4600 N. Kenmore July 1978 35
Hirsch and Artesian June 1976 37
Humboldt Park June 1976 39
Humboldt Park June 1976 41
Randolph and Canal November 1973 43
Three First National Plaza September 1978 45
Three First National Plaza September 1978 47
Grace & Sheridan June 1974 49
Randolph and Canal October 1977 51
Calumet River near Lake Michigan May 1976 55
700 S. Dearborn August 1978 53
LaSalle and Monroe September 1977 57
Montrose and Broadway July 1978 59
Lincoln Park October 1972 61
2600 N. Clark November 1985 63
Lincoln Park November 1973 65
Beacon & Wilson June 1978 67
900 W. Randolph October 1977 69
Washtenaw and Belmont November 1973 71
4400 S. Vincennes November 1977 73
Halsted and Fulton October 1977 75
700 N. Clark September 1974 77
Near Lakewood and Wellington July 1975 79
Arlington Park race track August 1976 81
Arlington Park race track August 1976 83
Arlington Park race track August 1976 85
333 W. Wacker Drive July 1981 87
Michigan and Randolph July 1975 89
Milwaukee Road railroad yards, Bensenville, Illinois July 1979 91
2600 N. Clark April 1977 93
2600 N. Clark April 1977 95
Maxwell and Newberry November 1975 97
3912 N. Cicero January 1987 99
Fullerton and Racine July 1980 101
2900 W. George October 1973 103
Barry, Clark, and Halsted October 1985 105
5800 N. Sheridan January 1976 107

About the Author

Richard Younker was born in Chicago and attended the University of Chicago, where he received his B.A. For the next ten years he worked as a mailman, sixth grade teacher, encyclopedia salesman, public aid caseworker, employment counselor, actor and singer. For the past thirteen years he has been a freelance photojournalist. Many of his photo essays have appeared in the *Chicago Sun-Times* and *Chicago Tribune* Sunday magazines. His previous books are *On Site*, about construction workers on a high-rise building, and *Street Signs Chicago*, about Chicago neighborhoods. He was one of five photographers who illustrated Studs Terkel's latest book, *Chicago*, and several of his pictures from that volume were screened on Charles Kuralt's "Sunday Morning" television program. He is the recipient of a Focus Infinity grant, which will enable him to document patterns of change in the Chicago area.